# Nottingham & Derbyshire
# TROLLEYBUSES

Barry M Marsden
*Series editor Robert J Harley*

MP Middleton Press

*FRONT COVER: A splendid shot of BUT 353, resplendent in its blue and white livery and pictured at the Nottingham terminus of the Notts and Derby system, on the corner of King Street. The trolleybus has been preserved and is now owned by Bournemouth HTC.*

*Published August 2005*

*ISBN 1 904474 63 2*

*© Middleton Press, 2005*

*Design Deborah Esher*

*Published by*
> *Middleton Press*
> *Easebourne Lane*
> *Midhurst, West Sussex*
> *GU29 9AZ*

*Tel: 01730 813169*
*Fax: 01730 812601*
*Email: info@middletonpress.co.uk*
*www.middletonpress.co.uk*

*Printed & bound by Biddles Ltd, Kings Lynn*

# CONTENTS

# INTRODUCTION AND ACKNOWLEDGEMENTS

By 1932 the Nottinghamshire and Derbyshire Traction Company's tramway system was on its last legs, and steps were taken to convert the undertaking to trolleybus operation. The Company had taken over the Ilkeston Corporation Tramway in 1916, with the intention of linking it to the main track at Heanor, but the union had never materialised. The Ilkeston trams had been replaced by motorbuses in early 1931 whilst the overhead was modified for trolleybus operation, and during 1932 17 single-deck trackless vehicles not only plied the old tram route, but pioneered a new service to Heanor, a total route mileage of some seven miles, connecting Ilkeston to the Notts and Derby system for the first time. By October of that year the main route from Ripley to Nottingham was also converted for trackless use and opened, served by 15 further double-deck trolleybuses which operated on the 15 mile/24km run. The railless period lasted just over 20 years before changing circumstances and other considerations led to a changeover to the all-powerful motor bus.

I have to thank a number of individuals and organisations for providing photographs of the system. Robin Symonds has granted me the use of his collection from the National Trolleybus Association, which includes the Harold Brearley Collection. Other material has come via Geoff Atkins, John Bircumshaw, C.Carter, Stanley King, the John Law Collection, Nigel Lemon, Steve Lockwood, Roy Marshall, the Heanor & District and Nuthall & District Local History Societies, Colin Routh and David Watts. I would like to extend my grateful thanks to all who have assisted me in my quest, and apologise for any inadvertent omissions in these acknowledgements. Ashley Bruce (who has produced an excellent CD-Rom on British Trolleybuses) has been most helpful, and has unearthed a rare image of the most elusive Guy single-decker purchased in 1932. I must also acknowledge my debt to Mike Jobling and the staff of Ilkeston Library for their uncomplaining and efficient identification of some of the more obscure localities along the route.

# GEOGRAPHICAL SETTING

The trolleybus route crossed a part rural, part industrial landscape, linking a series of towns and villages in south-east Derbyshire and north-west Nottinghamshire. It followed the path of the earlier tramline, apart from one divergence. At Basford on the northern outskirts of Nottingham, trackless vehicles ran down Nottingham and Mansfield Roads instead of the former tramline down Radford and Alfreton Roads. The terminus was situated in King Street. Today, the route has been vastly altered, with fresh building, roundabouts, new roads and one-way systems, whilst the once peaceful village of Nuthall has been cut in two by the M1 Motorway!

# HISTORICAL BACKGROUND

In 1928 the newly renamed Nottinghamshire & Derbyshire Traction Company decided to replace their ageing trams with trolleybuses on both the main Ripley-Nottingham line and the independent and unconnected Ilkeston subsidiary. The latter undertaking was the first to be converted; the last tramcar ran on the evening of 8th February 1931, and motorbuses took over the route whilst the overhead wiring was modified for trackless operation. The Station Road spur was abandoned, and the wiring was first restrung along the main line of the old tram track. This stretch was ready for use by 7th January 1932, and a new fleet of smart blue and cream front entrance single-deck 32-seat railless cars, based at the old Park Road Tram Depot, were ready to operate the new service. They consisted of six streamlined English Electrics (among the last of their breed), plus ten AEC 662Ts with half-cabs and dummy radiators, and a single Guy ex-demonstrator. Just why the company opted for such a disparate bunch of vehicles is unknown, but Mayor Richardson inaugurated the system by driving one of the AECs from the Town Hall, after which a civic party, augmented by Notts and Derby officials, attended dinner at the Rutland Hotel, presided over by the chairman of Balfour, Beatty, Sir Joseph Nall.

Between January and August 1932, the wires were extended north-west from the northern end of Bath Street along Heanor and Ilkeston Roads to link Ilkeston with the main route at Heanor. Another length of wire was pushed east from Heanor Road along Church Street to unite with the Cotmanhay Road terminus and provide an alternative way into Ilkeston via Heanor. The main expansion to Heanor, some three miles/4.8km long, was ready for use on 1st August, and from this date the trolleybuses operated two services: a direct one from Heanor which terminated outside the Rutland Hotel at the bottom of Bath Street, and a second which ran via Cotmanhay as far as Hallam Fields. These two routes were subsequently designated A3 and A2, whilst the Ripley-Nottingham run became A1.

Meanwhile work commenced in lifting the 15 miles of rail linking Ripley with Nottingham and revamping the overhead. Buses took over from the tramcars which were cut back to Heanor, leaving the trackless to temporarily service the Heanor-Ripley line. Track lifting and restringing of the running wire took until 4th October 1933, reaching as far east as Cinderhill, where Nottingham Corporation had recently extended its own wires. The whole network was then activated for railless running. The company had purchased 15 further trolleybuses, half-cab AEC661T rear-entrance double-deckers with MWCC metal bodies and seats for 55 passengers, and initially intended to ply the A1 route, though photographs show that the single-deckers often ventured along all parts of the system. The A1 line followed that of the old trams as far as Basford, when it diverted along Nottingham and Mansfield Roads, terminating at a new stop at the southern end of King Street via Milton Street and Upper Parliament Street, where the old trams had once ended their journey. The A1 service was 15 miles long, a comparatively speedy journey which ordinarily took 90 minutes and involved some 230 stops, giving it a claim to the longest through trolleybus run in Britain. Together with the Ilkeston extension, the whole undertaking was over 22 miles long.

At intervals along the line, trolley reversers or turning loops allowed for a number of short workings at busy periods, whilst at Heanor a one-way system permitted Ilkeston-bound buses to circle though the Market Place back onto Ilkeston Road. Trolley wheels were used throughout the life of the service, and on the more elevated and exposed stretches of the line frost was a winter problem. This was solved by using special frost-cutting trolley wheels with milled inside surfaces, which equipped the first vehicles out in the morning. In 1937 the six English Electric single-deckers were sold on to the Mexborough & Swinton Traction Company, where they gave many years of further service. Some of the AEC single-deckers, presumably due to the onset of World War 2, soldiered on until 1949. Between 1937 and 1942, 17 more AEC 661T 56 seat two-deckers were purchased for the company; these sported Weymann bodies with the more up-to-date full frontal design. In 1949, the 1933 AEC double-deckers were finally retired, being replaced by 15 British United Traction 9611Ts of the latest design. The Transport Manager recorded that the old AECs had performed sterling service; between them they had clocked up over ten million miles on the long inter-urban run. Each vehicle had averaged over 685,000 miles, which he believed to be a record.

Sadly the days of the Notts and Derby trackless era were by now numbered. The 1945 Labour Government had nationalised the power industry and Balfour, Beatty went to the British Electricity Authority (BEA) in 1948. BEA passed the undertaking on to the British Transport Commission (BTC), but with its large motorbus fleet, the BTC saw little point in running a small trolleybus system such as the Notts and Derby, especially as much of its equipment was in need of renewal. State ownership of the electricity industry meant that one of the main advantages of railless vehicles – cheap power from municipal and company-owned power stations – had gone. In 1952 the Notts and Derby (Discontinuance of Trolley Vehicles) Act spelt doom to the electric vehicles.

Unlike many trolleybus undertakings, there was to be no slow lingering death for the Notts and Derby, with gradual abandonments leading to a drawn-out closure. The entire facility closed down peremptorily on the evening of 25th April 1953. No formal ceremonies announced the end of the highly successful enterprise, the only concession to the termination being a series of three-halfpenny tickets overprinted in red with 'LAST TROLLEYBUS WEEK' and drawings of a tram and trolleybus on the back.

After the system had closed, all 32 trackless cars were sold on to Bradford Corporation, where they saw many more years' service. The sale was the largest ever of second-hand trolleybuses in Britain, and netted £62,500 for the company. The running wire brought in a further £23,438, and no less than 1,338 of the 1,679 traction poles were purchased by the various local authorities at £6 each to do duty as street lighting posts. David Watts has pointed out that the sale of the vehicles (though probably not the payment) was concluded on November 30th 1952, nearly five months before closure, whilst the overhead was purchased on March 30th, 1953. It would seem therefore that for the last few weeks Notts and Derby were running vehicles it may not strictly have owned under running wire it definitely did not own!

The fleet was replaced by 15 new Bristol motorbuses and 12 second-hand AECs from Mansfield, another Balfour, Beatty enterprise. Most of the railless were scrapped after their Bradford service, but three of the electric buses still remain. Two of the last batch of BUTs have been preserved, Nos 353 and 357. The former is owned by Bournemouth HTC (Hampshire Technology Centre), whilst the latter is in storage at Boughton near Ollerton, the property of Tom Bowden. Amazingly, one of the AEC single-deck half-cabs, No.307 is also stored at Boughton, the subject of a long-term renovation programme. It was rescued from Riddings in Derbyshire, where it had formerly done duty as a dwelling.

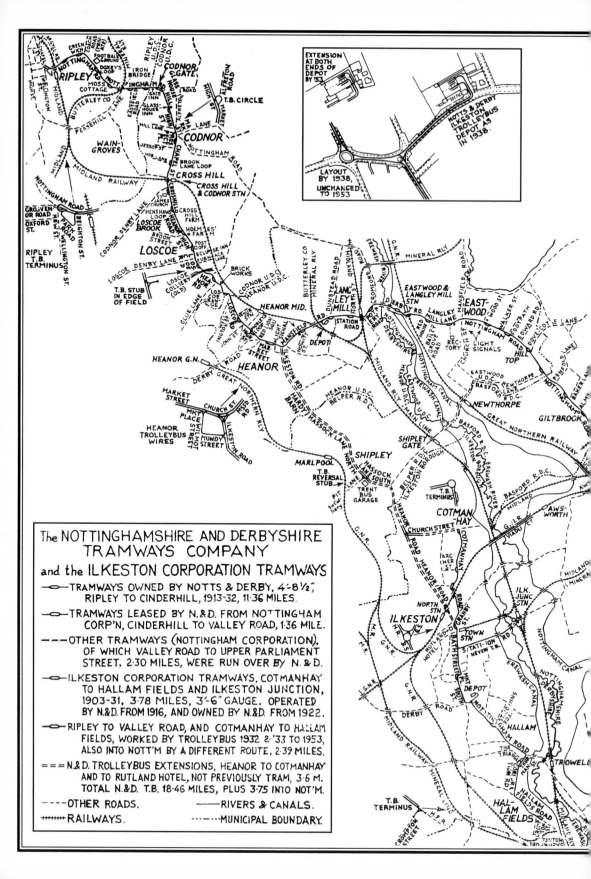

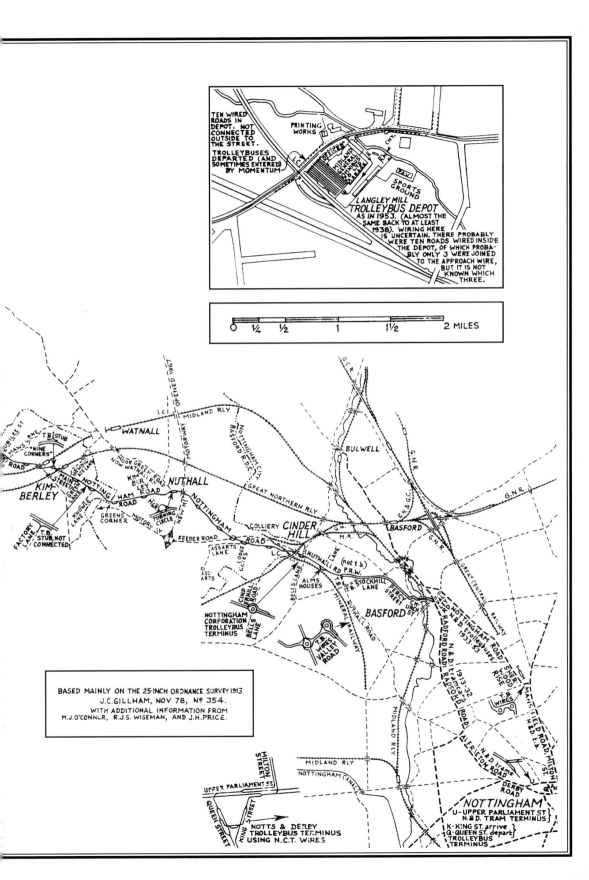

TEN WIRED ROADS IN DEPOT. NOT CONNECTED OUTSIDE TO THE STREET. TROLLEYBUSES DEPARTED (AND SOMETIMES ENTERED) BY MOMENTUM

PRINTING WORKS

MIDLAND GENERAL OMNIBUS CO. LTD.

SPORTS GROUND

PAV.

## LANGLEY MILL TROLLEYBUS DEPOT

AS IN 1953. (ALMOST THE SAME BACK TO AT LEAST 1938). WIRING HERE IS UNCERTAIN. THERE PROBABLY WERE TEN ROADS WIRED INSIDE THE DEPOT, OF WHICH PROBABLY ONLY 3 WERE JOINED TO THE APPROACH WIRE, BUT IT IS NOT KNOWN WHICH THREE.

0    ¼    ½    1    1½    2 MILES

WATNALL

BULWELL

KIMBERLEY

"NINE CORNERS"

NUTHALL

CINDER HILL

BASFORD

BASFORD

NOTTINGHAM CORPORATION TROLLEYBUS TERMINUS

VALLEY ROAD

BASED MAINLY ON THE 25-INCH ORDNANCE SURVEY 1913
J.C.GILLHAM, NOV 78, № 354.
WITH ADDITIONAL INFORMATION FROM
M.J.O'CONNOR, R.J.S.WISEMAN, AND J.H.PRICE.

MIDLAND RLY
NOTTINGHAM CANAL

MILTON STREET

UPPER PARLIAMENT ST.

KING STREET

QUEEN STREET

NOTTS & DERBY TROLLEYBUS TERMINUS USING N.C.T. WIRES

DERBY ROAD

NOTTINGHAM
U - UPPER PARLIAMENT ST
N.&D. TRAM TERMINUS
K - KING ST. arrive
Q - QUEEN ST. depart
TROLLEYBUS TERMINUS

# RIPLEY TERMINUS

1. One of the 1949 BUTs, no.344, pauses on the corner of Nottingham and Park Roads to allow passengers to disembark. The destination blind has already been reset for the return journey. Note the Ebenezer Wesleyan Chapel in the background, a notable Ripley landmark, now demolished.

2. The same spot on a much sunnier day in July 1952, as BUT 356 offloads a group of riders, and the driver chats to a lady acquaintance. The overhead wiring for the terminal loop can be seen at the top left of the photograph.

3. A single line of wiring allowed trolley vehicles to follow a circular route along Park Road and Beighton Street and reconnect with Nottingham Road for the 90 minute run back to Nottingham. Here in March 1953, BUTs 354 and 351 halt along the latter thoroughfare to await passengers for the return trip.

4. BUT 345 is nuzzled by a following trolleybus at the same venue, with a motorbus on the far left headed for Langley Mill on 8th October 1949. Note the single line of overhead carried here on bracket-arm poles.

5. Beighton Street is viewed from the opposite direction, with trackless and motorbuses jockeying for position along this narrow thoroughfare. The nearest trolleybus is BUT 357, the last of the 1949 batch, and the final Notts and Derby vehicle to enter service.

6. BUT 346 heads west into Ripley in April 1953 along Nottingham Road over the Midland Railway branch line. The chapel on the left of the picture was demolished shortly after the photograph was taken.

# CODNOR

7. One of the AEC double-deckers approaches the iron bridge at Codnor on its way into Ripley along Nottingham Road. The evocatively named Steam Mill Lane is just to the left of the trolleybus.

←——

8. A shot taken from the opposite direction near the same place picks out BUT 344 offloading schoolchildren along this then rural part of the route.

←——

9. In this early World War 2 scene, AEC 302, one of the batch of seven 1937 vintage buses, heads north through Codnor in August 1940. Note the white markings on the vehicle and roadside poles, and the mask on the nearside headlight. Much of the pleasant open country visible in this image has since suffered from extensive building.

10. Half-cab AEC 317, vintage 1933, is seen here passing over the Midland Railway bridge at the Cross Hill and Codnor Station, on a short working to the latter village. The overhead at this locality is carried on lengthy bracket-arm poles, presumably due to the telegraph wires on the opposite side of the roadway.

11. Passing through typical East Derbyshire scenery, BUT 345 climbs Crosshill Road as it heads south on its way to Loscoe and Heanor. Behind the trolleybus in this fine shot, Heanor Road climbs towards Codnor which is visible in the distance. Out of view on the left is Waingroves Road.

12. In the last week of service, April 1953, Nottingham-bound BUT 349 halts outside Cross Hill farm, just a little further up the road than the previous picture.

# HEANOR

13. Heanor was the hub of the Notts and Derby railless system, where the Ilkeston subsidiary line joined the main Nottingham – Ripley wires. Here BUT 348, on its way to Nottingham, halts at the shelter in Market Street, outside the Market Hotel. The wires joining the main overhead from Wilmot Street can be seen at the top left of the picture.

14. An excellent photograph looking south-east ——————▶
along Market Street picks out the tall tower of
St Lawrence's Church on the left, and AEC 342
on its way to Ripley. Wilmot Street is off to the
right, and the wiring connecting this side road
to the main system can be clearly seen above
the vehicle.

15. On the same side of the roadway as the
previous image, BUT 350 awaits trade for
Ripley. On the left is another trolleybus, parked
on Wilmot Street, ready for the return to Ilkeston.
On the far right in the Market Square is the Cosy
Cinema, which opened for business in 1923.

——————▶
16. AEC half-cab 320 waits at Wilmot Street for the return to Ilkeston against a backdrop of an
almost deserted Market Square on the A2 service to the latter town.

17. AEC 305 in the same spot on a much busier market day. Note the single-deck motor bus on the left, below the newly-established Fairs Restaurant.

18. A little further back on the same thoroughfare, AEC 339 awaits the conductor's bell before proceeding to Hallam Fields. The Cosy was screening 'Rawhide' and 'Wild Harvest' that week, the latter starring Alan Ladd and released in 1947, which should nicely date the photograph.

19. A busy day in Heanor, a shot taken looking in the opposite direction, with AEC 332 on the Hallam Fields run, and on the left AEC 341 embarking riders for Ripley. The crowds suggest another well-thronged market day.

20. A final look along the thoroughfare, as AEC 340 awaits the off on the A3 short run to the Rutland Hotel. The bus may be some time in starting, as the conductor sitting at the bottom left is either checking his waybill, or perhaps the latest scores.

21. On March 15th 1953, an enthusiasts' group travelling in BUT 343 waits in Market Street on a tour of the undertaking.

22. AEC 301 pauses outside the wall surrounding St Lawrence's Church on the direct route to the Rutland Hotel. The church perches at the end of an elevated spur, and the bus stands poised at the top of Church Street hill on the right.

23. From the opposite direction, BUT 350 climbs up the Church Street incline into Market Street, pursued by a distant motor bus. The Crown Hotel, just in shot on the right, was the successor to the earlier inn which was demolished to lay the tracks for the Notts and Derby Tramway in 1913. Ilkeston Road can just be discerned on the right, with the two-way overhead linking Ilkeston to the main wires.

24. On a short-working to Loscoe, single-deck AEC 311 pulls out of Ilkeston Road onto Market Street. The building behind, once the premises of Machin and Hartwell, is now the Heanor Antiques Centre. On the left is the Crown Hotel, now bizarrely redesignated 'Que Sera.'

25. AEC 302 pauses along Ilkeston Road in March 1953, en route to the Rutland Hotel on the short A3 service.

26. Further along the same thoroughfare AEC 337 halts outside 'Carisbrooke', 25 Ilkeston Road, on the right. The house still bears the same name, but has been much altered. The Esso petrol station behind the vehicle is now a branch of Manor Pharmacy.

27. An end-of-service enthusiasts' tour in BUT 346 halts on Heanor Road for a photo call on the way into Ilkeston. In one of the back gardens of a house along this thoroughfare is the lower saloon body of an Ilkeston tram, long doing duty as a shed.

28. In low evening sunshine BUT 346 heads north-west along Heanor Road on a short-working to Shipley, though the indicator blind incorrectly shows the route as A1. The trackless, here chased by an overtaking motorbus in the gathering gloom, has just passed the Ilkeston Borough boundary, marked by the sign on the right. The photograph shows clearly the twin pole and span wire arrangement on this part of the system.

29. AEC 304, on the A3 run, poses at the most south-easterly point of Heanor Road, opposite Granby Street in March 1953, just before commencing its run back to Heanor.

# ILKESTON :
# COTMANHAY TERMINUS

30. 'Oh what a tangled web we weave…' Once a quiet part of the route, this 1950 shot, looking north, shows the new roundabout and the considerable development of the once rural locality. The recently laid Skeavington's Lane, named after the farm in the right distance, is lined by modern prefabs. Church Street is to the left, Bridge Street to the right, and Cotmanhay Road in the foreground. The mesh of overhead wires includes a loop for vehicles using the roundabout and twin sets of wires at the top right, the innermost pair deployed for trolleybuses halting at the terminus.

31. Shadowed by a motorcyclist, AEC 339 utilises the roundabout loop to turn into Cotmanhay Road on the A2 Hallam Fields service in April 1953. The railings surrounding the Methodist Chapel can be seen at the bottom right. Note the open vista still existing behind the trolleybus.

32. A smart-looking AEC 301 halts at the terminus, using the outer pair of wires. The façade of the chapel can be seen behind the rear of the bus, and open countryside still prevails in the distance.

# GRANBY STREET

33. This short thoroughfare linked Cotmanhay Road with the foot of Bath Street. In this view AEC 303 heads south-west for Ilkeston town centre and Hallam Fields terminus, passing typical rows of terraces along the route.

# BATH STREET

34. In this 1952 scene one of the BUTs uses the turning circle at the junction of Heanor Road, Bath Street and Granby Street for the return journey to Heanor. Granby Street is behind the trackless, with the Bath Street incline to the right. Behind the trolleybus is the Mundy Arms.

35. March 1953 and AEC 336 loads up outside the Rutland Arms at the northern end of Bath Street on its way to Cotmanhay. The vehicle still maintains a clean and neat appearance, despite the impending end of the trolleybus era.

36. At the very top of Bath Street AEC 332, on a short-working to White Lion Square, disembarks passengers at the north end of the Market Place. Barton's Greengrocers is visible between the rear of the trackless and the traction pole.

37. On the opposite side of the road the same vehicle picks up trade as it heads downhill on the way to Shipley, with the Market Inn behind. In taking this original colour photograph, Mr. C. Carter must have been chagrined as the mother and daughter on the right threatened to spoil his shot!

38. In the same spot, AEC 336, with some damage visible around the driver's door, stops on its way to Heanor. No less than three pubs, within close proximity of each other, provided stimulation for the weary traveller on this part of the route!

39. AEC 339 poses at the same place, but at a later date judging by the altered sign on the Sir John Warren Pub on the left. The third member of the trio of inns was the King's Head, situated immediately behind the rear end of the bus, above the parked motorcycle.

# SOUTH STREET

40. English Electric 304, Cotmanhay bound, climbs north up South Street sometime in the mid-1930s, running under wiring supported by bracket poles. In the left distance is White Lion Square, and the two-storey premises of the Derbyshire and Nottinghamshire Electric Power Company. A third storey was added to the building in 1936-7.

# WHITE LION SQUARE

41. By the late 1930s the Square bore a vastly different appearance than it had in the tramway era. Two roundabouts had been constructed, and the Derby and Notts Power Company had elevated their headquarters on the right by adding another floor. Derby Road is at the bottom left, Park Road leads off above it, whilst Nottingham Road heads off at centre right. The turning loop and other wiring shows up clearly, whilst the masked road signs hint at preparations for war.

42. AEC 303 halts on the south side of the Square in March 1953, with the now-demolished Traveller's Rest pub behind the vehicle. This whole area suffered wholesale demolition in 1991 for the huge roundabout now situated in this locality as part of the bypass which cuts through the town on its eastern side.

43. Single-deck AEC 315 is here pictured turning into the Square from Nottingham Road on a short-working to Loscoe. Park Road leads off to the left, from which the tower waggon behind the trolleybus has obviously hailed, with a linesman busily checking the web of overhead wiring at this point.

# PARK ROAD DEPOT

44. This view of the façade of the Depot dates from the tram era, but it changed little during the subsequent railless period. The car shed can be seen at the extreme right, and trolleybuses exited from right to left along the frontage of this now-demolished edifice.

45. A lineup of the smartly-liveried AEC half-cabs taken at the depot during the inauguration of the Ilkeston service in early 1932. The lines of the front-entrance single-deckers with English-Electric bodywork, can be appreciated in this side view.

46. A frontal shot of the same vehicles in brand-new paint includes nos 309, left, flanked on the right by 308 and 310. No fleet numbers have as yet been applied. Note the varying destinations on the blinds, and the elaborate lining-out on the liveries.

47. AEC 311 is here seen entering the Depot via Park Road, sporting WHITE LION SQUARE on its destination blind. Advertising boards now sully the rugged lines of these vehicles, whilst the front nearside tyre looks decidedly bereft of tread in this shot!

# NOTTINGHAM ROAD

48. A familiar image, which shows EE 302 heading north-west up Nottingham Road at its junction with Cavendish Road in May 1935. Again the elegant colour scheme of the vehicle shows up well. Note the feeder cables boosting power to the overhead, here carried on twin poles and span wire, for the uphill climb. Another trolleybus can be seen through the rear windows of the bus. (G.H.F.Atkins/John Banks coll.)

# THURMAN STREET

49. Further south-east down Nottingham Road, EE 301 turns into Thurman Street on the final stages of the run to Hallam Fields terminus. Brook Street can be seen behind the single-decker. (G.H.F.Atkins/John Banks coll.)

# HALLAM FIELDS TERMINUS

50. AEC 305 is here seen arriving at Hallam Fields in April 1953, pausing outside the shops on the north-east side of the road. The trolleybus is about to use the reverser for the return to town.

←———

51. AEC 304 has just swung into Crompton Road, alongside St Bartholomew's Church, in July 1952, before reversing back into Hallam Fields Road. The wiring for the reverser shows up clearly against the sky.

←———

52. Another trackless, AEC 335, occupies the same position in this picture, which has been taken from the opposite direction, and which again picks out the wiring for the reverser. The tower of St Bartholomew's can be seen on the right. It was damaged by bombs dropped from a Zeppelin aiming for the nearby Stanton Ironworks in 1916. Disestablished in 1969, the building is now occupied by a removal firm.

53. Destination blind reset for HEANOR, AEC 305 has reversed back onto the main road for its return journey. Note the wide sweep of open country behind the vehicle. To the right of the telephone booth alongside the shop on the left can be seen a plume of smoke from a passing locomotive.

54. AEC 336 replaces no. 305 in this scene, taken in July 1952, on a warm day judging by the driver's raised split windscreen. Stanton village and ironworks is off to the right along Crompton Road, according to the signpost fixed to the traction post.

55. A final look down a deserted Hallam Fields Road as the driver and conductor of AEC 333 have a final chat before setting off for Cotmanhay. The distant bridge crosses the River Erewash, the boundary between Derbyshire and Nottinghamshire.

56. Neatly dated by the 'G.R.' motif and LONG LIVE THE KING, AEC half-cab 331 parades at the Langley Mill Depot, bedizened with bunting, flags and coloured light bulbs for the Coronation of King George VI in May 1937.

57. Ready for a private tour, AEC 301 poses in the main garage alongside a string of other double-deckers arrayed in line-astern in 1953. Note also the single-deck bus in the left-hand distance.

58. A fine shot of the old and the new in the Depot yard on May Day 1949 as the line of brand-new BUT 9611Ts prepare to take over from the ageing 1933 AEC half-cabs on the right, which have been shorn of their trolleybooms and electrical equipment. Between them the latter vehicles had clocked up over ten million miles on the system.

59. BUT 344 has just parked opposite the Depot along Mansfield Road in what was then fairly open countryside. The trolleybus is heading east for Nottingham.

60. In a shot dated to 1933, a pristine AEC half-cab 317, the first of the 1933 batch, heads through the village along Mansfield Road on a possible proving run. Note the elaborate and attractive livery applied to the brand-new trackless.

61. Perhaps a dozen years later no. 327 poses at the same spot, having ended its short-working to Langley Mill, showing the effects of anno domini and hard work. The colour scheme has been much modified and the trolleybus looks more than a little tired. The photograph gives a good view of the wiring at this point.

62. A splendid image of the same vehicle entering the depot via Mansfield Road. Though the depot was wired up to enable trolleybuses to get into the yard, there was no exit wiring, and buses departed on momentum alone.

# EASTWOOD

63. AEC half-cab 321 is seen here running south-east through Nottingham Road, Eastwood, home of D.H. Lawrence, who had once written with affection of the 'Ripley Trams'. Note that the upper blind is blank; it is believed that the route letters and numbers were not displayed until 1936.

64. BUT 351 heads towards Nottingham along the same road, passing the Midland Bank on the right, in a photograph taken some time in the early 1950s.

# KIMBERLEY

65. Two of the double-decker half-cabs pass each other along a narrow Main Street, Kimberley in the mid-1930s. AEC 324 heads towards Ripley, passing the Queen's Head inn on the left. Between the vehicles at cab level, is the low iron bridge which carried the Great Northern Railway across the main road.

# NUTHALL

66. One of the BUTs pauses along a pleasant Nottingham Road, lined with neat suburban villas, at Nuthall, picking up trade for the return trip to Derbyshire, sometime near the end of the electric service. These quiet, smooth-running buses would be greatly missed in the face of the noisier, smellier motor vehicles which replaced them.

67. A well-loaded BUT 344 passes St Patrick's Church, Nuthall, on its way to Nottingham in 1952. The picture gives a good view of the overhead wiring along this part of the route.

68. AEC half-cab 328 is here pictured on Nottingham Road, halfway between Nuthall and Cinderhill. Behind the wide swathe of grass verge on the left was Nuthall Temple, a Jacobean mansion demolished in 1929, sometime before this image was recorded.

69. A well-laden BUT 354 halts on Nuthall Road, Cinderhill, on the outskirts of suburban Nottingham.

70. BUT 347, lacking its fleet number, pauses to offload a mother and child on Nuthall Road on its way to Ripley on 6th April 1953, at the terminus for Nottingham Corporation trolleybuses coming from the city. The Corporation trackless on the left was on the 41 Service which, like the Notts and Derby also terminated at King Street. The wiring for the turning circle for these vehicles can be seen at the top left of the photograph.

71. Taken from the opposite direction, half-cab AEC 328 is seen negotiating the roundabout at the Cinderhill terminus for Nottingham Corporation trolleybuses. In the background is the GNR bridge spanning Nuthall Road. Bell's Lane is to the left, and Cinderhill Road on the right in a shot probably taken at the same time as 68 and 73.

# BASFORD

72. A fine shot of AEC 337 climbing a cobbled Church Street on the way out of Basford. The trolleybus is about to turn right into Alpine Street, with Cinderhill the next stop.

73. Descending into Church Street, AEC half-cab 328 pauses in front of the Swan, now the White Swan, passing a waiting horse-and-cart on its way into Nottingham. At Basford the Notts and Derby trolleybus route diverged from the former tramline, which headed down Radford Road. The trackless went along Valley Road and entered the city via Nottingham Road, further to the east.

# NOTTINGHAM:
## VALLEY ROAD

74. BUT 343 heads along Valley Road, having just crossed over the Midland Railway bridge, visible behind the trolleybus in an image dating to December 1952. On the right is Basford Gasworks, with the Five Ways Garage alongside Vernon Road. (G.H.F.Atkins/John Banks coll.)

75. Opposite the former gasworks, BUT 343, the first of the 1949 newcomers, halts for a picture call at a roundabout on an enthusiasts' outing, along part of the old tram route. The Shoulder of Mutton pub visible on the extreme right, has since been demolished.

76. AEC half-cab 322 moves along Valley Road in September 1948 on a short-working to Hill Top on the south-eastern outskirts of Eastwood, chased by a brace of motorcyclists. (G.H.F. Atkins/John Banks coll.)

77. In an image dated April 1934, one of the 1933 AECs is seen outside the National Provincial Bank at the junction between Valley Road and Nottingham Road which is in the right foreground. Perversely the trolleybus is advertising the merits of the Nottingham Savings Bank!

# NOTTINGHAM ROAD

78. BUT 352 glides smoothly down the long sweep of a cobbled Nottingham Road on the way into the city in a scene which must date to the early 1950s. Note the overhead turning circle for Nottingham trolleybuses; the board in front of the Star Garage on the left indicates a trolleybus service to Vernon Road.

79. Another Nottingham Road vista, dated April 1953, as AEC 340 progresses towards Langley Mill on another curtailed service at the end of the trackless era.

# GREGORY BOULEVARD

80. Single-decker AEC 306, on the long run to Ripley, turns into Gregory Boulevard from Mansfield Road, on a wet and miserable day, in November 1933. Note the Nottingham Corporation balcony tram on the left on its way north to Arnold, and the bus stop sign on the right which uses the term 'Railless'. Was this a term introduced by Manager Walter Marks, who had also applied it to trolleybuses during his service in Chesterfield?
(G.H.F.Atkins/John Banks coll.)

81. AEC half-cab 319 is pictured at more-or-less the same venue in February 1934, again on the Ripley service. Of particular interest is the elaborate early paint scheme on these buses, which involved some ornate lining-out.

82. On the opposite side of the road BUT 333 is about to turn into Mansfield Road from Gregory Boulevard, the fine tree-lined avenue seen on the left, in a photograph taken in July 1949, when the BUTs were relatively new. (G.H.F.Atkins/John Banks coll.)

# MANSFIELD ROAD

83. At the same spot, marked by the telephone booth on the right, AEC 301 also heads for the city centre down Mansfield Road. Note the variant lettering style on the lower indicator blind.

84. Ripley-bound BUT 356 proceeds north out of the city along Mansfield Road in March 1953, with the tower of the now-defunct Victoria Railway Station visible in the right-hand distance. The Pentecostal Church on the left is advertising a visit by the American faith healer, Valdez.

# CANNING CIRCUS

85. Not a recognisable part of the Notts and Derby railless route, though their earlier trams knew it well as they plied this run until 1932. Here BUT 343, on an enthusiasts' tour, uses Nottingham City wiring to progress through Canning Circus, flanked by Nottingham motorbuses to the right and left.

# MILTON STREET

86. BUT 351, halted outside the Victoria Station on Milton Street, is closely followed by a Nottingham Corporation trackless and a city motorbus as it offloads passengers.

87. A little further along Milton Street, BUT 349 is also pictured outside the station in August 1950. The driver has already altered the indicator blind for the return journey. The lower part of the elaborate station tower can be seen at the top left of the picture.

88. AEC half-cab 320 seems to be experiencing some difficulties as it poses, trolleybooms down, in Trinity Square, just off Milton Street in the background, into which it appears to have been pushed. The crew behind seem to be trying to manoeuvre the booms by means of long poles. On the left is the Victoria Station Hotel, now the Nottingham Hilton.

89. BUT 353 stops along the southern end of Milton Street, blind already reset for the return to Ripley, followed by a city motorbus. After subsequent service in Bradford, this vehicle is now preserved by the Bournemouth HTC.

90. AEC 338 moves south out of Milton Street, alongside the Milton's Head inn on the final stage of its journey into Nottingham in July 1949. It is turning right into Parliament Street on its way to King Street and the Notts and Derby terminus.

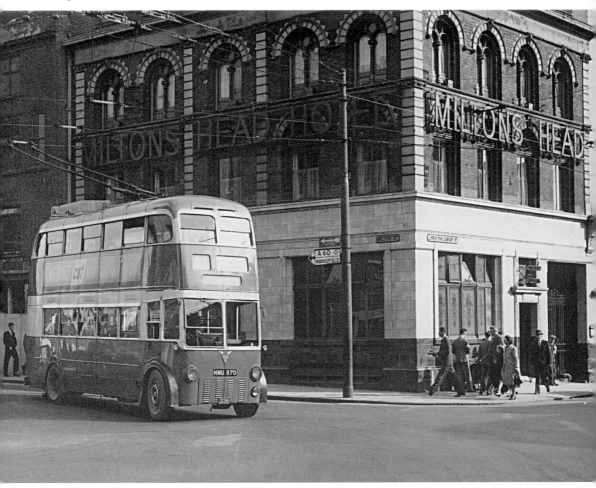

# KING STREET TERMINUS

91. BUT 345 halts a little way down King Street on a cool, wet end-of-September day in 1952 with its return destination already in place. At this time the system had less than seven months to run.

———▶

92. Another King Street view shows BUT 343, on an enthusiasts' excursion, ranged alongside Nottingham 495, another BUT from the same stable as 343, but fitted with a Roe body. The latter trolleybus was plying the 40 Service to Wilford Road.

———▶

93. Notts and Derby vehicles stopped over at a lay-by just outside the Prudential offices at the corner of King and Queen Streets. Here AEC half-cab 318 awaits passengers as driver and conductor compare notes in front of the vehicle in appropriate summer rig.

94. Much film must have been exposed by enthusiasts at this venue over the years. Here BUT 346 awaits the time for departure on a deserted-looking street. The line of overhead curving round into Queen Street can be clearly seen in this view, which reveals driver and conductor keeping very much to themselves!

95. A much sunnier day as an immaculate-looking BUT 354, lacking its service number, lays over whilst various bus crews chew the fat on the left. The date is June 1949.

96. BUT 351, again lacking its fleet number, cosies up to Nottingham 49, a venerable Brush-bodied Ransomes dating from 1932, and only a year away from retirement. The latter trolleybus was plying the route 41 Cinderhill run. (G.H.F.Atkins/John Banks coll.)

97. Appalling conditions prevail, as an AEC prepares to move off from a snowy King Street on a winter's evening for the trip back to Ripley. Note the effect that snow and ice had on the overhead wiring. Frost was another winter problem which was only solved by fitting special trolleyheads with milled inner surfaces to cut away the icy coating. (G.H.F.Atkins/John Banks coll.)

# QUEEN STREET

98. The return to Ripley began in Queen Street, where the wiring seen at the top right carried the Notts and Derby vehicles round the curve and up the thoroughfare. In this view the trackless seen on the left is a Nottingham one. Along this street the overhead was carried on bracket-arm poles.

99. At the top of Queen Street trolleybuses turned right along Parliament Street to gain access back into Milton Street on the route out of Nottingham. Here, BUT 344 pauses under the watching eye of the law in April 1953 for the go ahead. The quick-striding gentleman on the left seems keen to enter the Elite Cinema for a view of Gene Kelly in 'The Devil Makes Three.'

100.Chaos reigns supreme at the top of Queen Street as another elderly Nottingham trolleybus, Leyland 416 of 1935 vintage, attempts to get past a stalled Notts & Derby trolleybus, whose crew are attempting some juggling with their trolleypole. A city motorbus on the right is also seeking to get in on the act.

# PARLIAMENT STREET

101. BUT 343, trolleys down, is on an enthusiasts' trip (see pictures 21, 75, 85 and 92) along the system. It is halted outside the Elite Cinema, with King Street visible on the far left. Gene Tierney's 'Laura' dates from 1944, but was obviously enjoying a re-run at this time.

# FINAL DAY

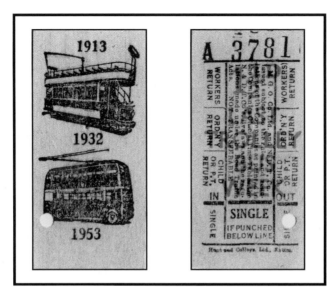

102. Practically nothing was done to celebrate the passing of the trolleybuses in April 1953. The only concession was to overprint the threehalfpenny tickets in red for the final week. On the reverse these tickets bore drawings of Notts and Derby trams and trackless, with the appropriate dates.

103. The final day in Ripley, as one of the BUTs and its crew pose on Beighton Street, just before commencing the 15 mile trip to Nottingham.

104. On the same last day of trackless operation, another BUT passes through Nuthall along Nottingham Road en route to the city.

105. The end of it all, as a gleaming and empty BUT 347 prepares for the final electric-powered journey to Ripley on the night of April 25th 1953, from a deserted King Street, a poignant memorial to the 20 year reign of the speedy and efficient trolleybus fleet, which is still remembered with affection by all those who travelled on it. (G.H.F.Atkins/John Banks coll.)

# FLEET VEHICLES

106. The first trolleybuses in the Notts and Derby fleet were six smart and streamlined English Electric single-deckers, which first operated in Ilkeston. Here one of the vehicles is photographed at the English Electric works before receiving its registration plate and fleet number. The livery looks lighter than the later blue, and the early logo is interesting, and presumably short-lived. The AEC single-deckers (see picture 45) carried the NDT letters enclosed in a circular belt from the start.

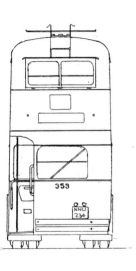

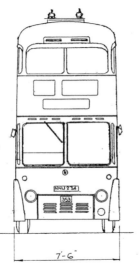

## NOTTS & DERBY TRACTION CO.
## 2 AXLE D/DECK TROLLEYBUS

| Body: Weymann 1949. Chassis: BUT 9611T. Fleet No. 343 - 357. | Scale: 4   mm = 1Foot. |
|---|---|

### DRAWING No. TB50

SCALE FEET   0  1  2  3  4  5  6  7  8  9  10  11  12

7'-6"

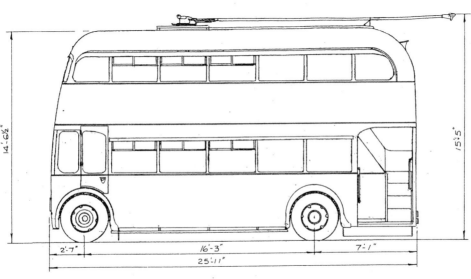

14'-6½"      15'-5"

2'-7"        16'-3"        7'-1"

25'-11"

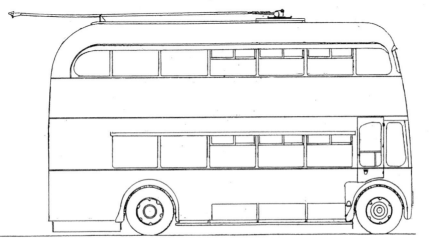

107. Rare indeed is this possibly unique, picture of the single Guy BT32 demonstrator bought by the company. No other photographs of this particular railless appear to exist, and its fate is unrecorded. The venue here is problematical, and the vehicle may well have been superimposed on a suitable backdrop.

108. Ten single-deck AEC 662T half-cabs joined the other trolleybuses in 1932. Here no. 313 is seen heading for Ripley along Milton Street, Nottingham, in December 1934.
(G.H.F.Atkins/John Banks coll.)

109. In this photograph one of the AECs has its dummy bonnet opened to reveal the electric motor behind. These vehicles always bore the appearance of motorbuses, with trolleybooms added seemingly as an afterthought!

110. The first double-deckers in the fleet were 15 rugged-looking AEC 661Ts (nos 317-331) with MCCW bodies complete with dummy bonnet and radiator.

111. No.326, in its elaborate original colour scheme, is seen operating in Nottingham early during its service life.

112. AEC 661T 300 was the first of the seven more modern-looking Notts and Derby fleet, with its Weymann bodywork. It entered service in 1937.

113. AEC 334 was one of the batch of ten 1941-42 trolleybuses delivered to the undertaking. It is seen here at the Cotmanhay terminus in Ilkeston.

114. The last fleet augmentation took place in 1949, when 15 BUT 9611Ts replaced the ageing 1933 AECs. Here no. 343, first of the replacements, is pictured at Hallam Fields terminus.

# FURTHER SERVICE

115. The six Notts and Derby EE single-deckers were sold to Mexborough and Swinton in 1937. They became nos 64-69 in their fleet. No. 65 (ex-301) is pictured just before its retirement in 1950.

116. All 32 double-decker trolleybuses were sold to Bradford in 1953, and were renumbered 580-96 and 760-74. Here Bradford 592 (ex-338) passes through the city centre on its way to Thornbury.

117. Bradford 773 (ex-356) is here seen on its way to Bankfoot. The last of the ex-Notts and Derby buses were pensioned off in 1968. Ironically the AECs outlasted the later BUTs, which were taken out of service ten years earlier.

# SURVIVORS

118, 119. Amazingly one of the trolleybuses to survive was AEC single-decker 307 which was found behind the Victoria pub at Riddings in Derbyshire, in use as a dwelling. It is seen here at Sandtoft, and is now in storage at Boughton near Ollerton, the property of Tom Bowden.

120. The only Notts and Derby vehicle to be restored in its original livery is no. 353, now preserved by the Bournemouth HTC. This photograph, taken in 1968 by Nigel Lemon, shows it stored at the Blue Bus Garage at Willington, Derbyshire, in June 1968. Note the destination blinds, which reveal a mixture of Bradford and Derby termini!

# MP Middleton Press

Easebourne Lane, Midhurst, West Sussex.
GU29 9AZ   Tel:01730 813169

EVOLVING THE ULTIMATE RAIL ENCYCLOPEDIA

www.middletonpress.co.uk   email:info@middletonpress.co.uk
A-0 906520   B-1 873793   C-1 901706   D-1 904474

**OOP** Out of Print at time of printing - Please check current availability   **BROCHURE AVAILABLE SHOWING NEW TITLES**